A KIND OF ALASKA

(from Other Places)

A Play

by Harold Pinter

‖SAMUEL FRENCH‖

samuelfrench.co.uk

Copyright © 1982 by Askerdale Limited
All Rights Reserved

A KIND OF ALASKA is fully protected under the copyright laws of the British Commonwealth, including Canada, the United States of America, and all other countries of the Copyright Union. All rights, including professional and amateur stage productions, recitation, lecturing, public reading, motion picture, radio broadcasting, television and the rights of translation into foreign languages are strictly reserved.

ISBN 978-0-573-12129-6

www.samuelfrench.co.uk

www.samuelfrench.com

For Amateur Production Enquiries

United Kingdom and World
excluding north america

plays@samuelfrench.co.uk

020 7255 4302/01

Each title is subject to availability from Samuel French, depending upon country of performance.

CAUTION: Professional and amateur producers are hereby warned that *A KIND OF ALASKA* is subject to a licensing fee. Publication of this play does not imply availability for performance. Both amateurs and professionals considering a production are strongly advised to apply to the appropriate agent before starting rehearsals, advertising, or booking a theatre. A licensing fee must be paid whether the title is presented for charity or gain and whether or not admission is charged.

The professional rights in this play are controlled by Judy Daish Associates Ltd, 2 St Charles Pl, London W10 6EG.

No one shall make any changes in this title for the purpose of production. No part of this book may be reproduced, stored in a retrieval system, or transmitted in any form, by any means, now known or yet to be invented, including mechanical, electronic, photocopying, recording, videotaping, or otherwise, without the prior written permission of the publisher. No one shall upload this title, or part of this title, to any social media websites.

The right of Harold Pinter to be identified as author of this work has been asserted in accordance with Section 77 of the Copyright, Designs and Patents Act 1988.

THINKING ABOUT PERFORMING A SHOW?

There are thousands of plays and musicals available to perform from Samuel French right now, and applying for a licence is easier and more affordable than you might think

---

From classic plays to brand new musicals, from monologues to epic dramas, there are shows for everyone.

Plays and musicals are protected by copyright law, so if you want to perform them, the first thing you'll need is a licence. This simple process helps support the playwright by ensuring they get paid for their work and means that you'll have the documents you need to stage the show in public.

Not all our shows are available to perform all the time, so it's important to check and apply for a licence before you start rehearsals or commit to doing the show.

LEARN MORE & FIND THOUSANDS OF SHOWS

Browse our full range of plays and musicals, and find out more about how to license a show

www.samuelfrench.co.uk/perform

Talk to the friendly experts in our Licensing team for advice on choosing a show and help with licensing

plays@samuelfrench.co.uk   020 7387 9373

Acting Editions
BORN TO PERFORM

Playscripts designed from the ground up to work the way you do in rehearsal, performance and study

Larger, clearer text for easier reading

Wider margins for notes

Performance features such as character and props lists, sound and lighting cues, and more

+ CHOOSE A SIZE AND STYLE TO SUIT YOU

STANDARD EDITION

Our regular paperback book at our regular size

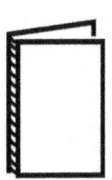

SPIRAL-BOUND EDITION

The same size as the Standard Edition, but with a sturdy, easy-to-fold, easy-to-hold spiral-bound spine

LARGE EDITION

A4 size and spiral bound, with larger text and a blank page for notes opposite every page of text – perfect for technical and directing use

| LEARN MORE | samuelfrench.co.uk/actingeditions

**Other plays by HAROLD PINTER
published and licensed by Samuel French**

Celebration

The Birthday Party

The Caretaker

The Dumb Waiter

Family Voices (from the collection *Other Places*)

The Homecoming

A Kind of Alaska (from the collection *Other Places*)

The Lover

Mixed Doubles

Mountain Language

A Night Out

One for the Road (from the collection *Other Places*)

One to Another

The Room

A Slight Ache

Victoria Station (from the collection *Other Places*)

**Other plays by HAROLD PINTER
licensed by Samuel French**

Apart from That

Ashes to Ashes

The Basement

Betrayal

The Black and White

The Dwarfs

The Hothouse

Landscape

Last To Go

Monologue

Moonlight

The New World Order

Night School

No Man's Land

Old Times

Party Time

Precisely

Press Conference

Request Stop

Silence

Tess

That's All

That's Your Trouble

Trouble in the Works

FIND PERFECT PLAYS TO PERFORM AT
www.samuelfrench.co.uk/perform

ABOUT THE AUTHOR

Harold Pinter was born in London in 1930. He lived with Antonia Fraser from 1975 until his death on Christmas Eve 2008. (They were married in 1980).

After studying at the Royal Academy of Dramatic Art and the Central School of Speech and Drama, he worked as an actor under the stage name David Baron. Following his success as a playwright, he continued to act under his own name, on stage and screen. He last acted in 2006 when he appeared in Beckett's *Krapp's Last Tape* at the Royal Court Theatre, directed by Ian Rickson.

He wrote twenty-nine plays including *The Birthday Party, The Dumb Waiter, A Slight Ache, The Hothouse, The Caretaker, The Collection, The Lover, The Homecoming, Old Times, No Man's Land, Betrayal, A Kind of Alaska, One For The Road, The New World Order, Moonlight* and *Ashes to Ashes*. Sketches include *The Black and White, Request Stop, That's your Trouble, Night, Precisely, Apart From that* and the recently rediscovered, *Umbrellas*.

He directed twenty-seven theatre productions, including James Joyce's *Exiles*, David Mamet's *Oleanna*, seven plays by Simon Gray (one of which was *Butley* in 1971 which he directed the film of three years later) and many of his own plays including his last, *Celebration*, paired with his first, *The Room* at The Almeida Theatre, London in the spring of 2000.

He wrote twenty-one screenplays including *The Pumpkin Eater, The Servant, The Go-Between, The French Lieutenant's Woman* and *Sleuth*.

In 2005 he received the Nobel Prize for Literature. Other awards include the Companion of Honour for services to Literature, the Legion D'Honneur, the European Theatre Prize the Laurence Olivier Award and the Moliere D'Honneur for lifetime achievement. In 1999 he was made a Companion of Literature by the Royal Society of Literature. Harold Pinter was awarded eighteen honorary degrees.

A Kind of Alaska was inspired by *Awakenings* by Oliver Sacks M.D., first published in 1973 by Gerald Duckworth and Co.

In the winter of 1916–17, there spread over Europe, and subsequently over the rest of the world, an extraordinary epidemic illness which presented itself in innumerable forms — as delirium, mania, trances, coma, sleep, insomnia, restlessness, and states of Parkinsonism. It was eventually identified by the great physician Constantin von Economo and named by him *encephalitis lethargica*, or sleeping sickness.

Over the next ten years almost five million people fell victim to the disease of whom more than a third died. Of the survivors some escaped almost unscathed, but the majority moved into states of deepening illness. The worst-affected sank into singular states of "sleep" — conscious of their surroundings but motionless, speechless, and without hope or will, confined to asylums or other institutions.

Fifty years later, with the development of the remarkable drug L-DOPA, they erupted into life once more.

A KIND OF ALASKA

First performed as part of the triple bill *Other Places** in the Cottesloe auditorium of the National Theatre, London, on 14th October, 1982, with the following cast:

DEBORAH	Judi Dench
HORNBY	Paul Rogers
PAULINE	Anna Massey

Directed by Peter Hall
Designed by John Bury

**Family Voices, One for the Road* and *Victoria Station* are available separately in Acting Editions published by Samuel French.

To Mick Goldstein

A woman in a white bed. Mid-forties. She sits up against high-banked pillows, stares ahead. A table and two chairs. A window. A man in a dark suit sits at the table. Early sixties.

The woman's eyes move. She slowly looks about her. Her gaze passes over the man and on. He watches her. She stares ahead, still. She whispers.

DEBORAH Something is happening.

Silence.

HORNBY Do you know me?

Silence.

Do you recognize me?

Silence.

Can you hear me?

She does not look at him.

DEBORAH Are you speaking?

HORNBY Yes.

Pause.

Do you know who I am?

Pause.

Who am I?

DEBORAH No one hears what I say. No one is listening to me.

Who am I?

You are no one.

Pause.

Who is it? It is miles away. The rain is falling. I will get wet.

Pause.

I can't get to sleep. The dog keeps turning about. I think he's dreaming. He wakes me up, but not himself up. He's my best dog though. I talk French.

Pause.

HORNBY I would like you to listen to me.

Pause.

You have been asleep for a very long time. You have now woken up. We are here to care for you.

Pause.

You have been asleep for a very long time. You are older, although you do not know that. You are still young, but older.

Pause.

DEBORAH Something is happening.

HORNBY You have been asleep. You have awoken. Can you hear me? Do you understand me?

She looks at him for the first time.

DEBORAH Asleep?

Pause.

I do not remember that.

Pause.

People have been looking at me. They have been touching me. I spoke, but I don't think they heard what I said.

Pause.

What language am I speaking? I speak French, I know that. Is this French?

Pause.

I've not seen Daddy today. He's funny. He makes me laugh. He runs with me. We play with balloons.

Pause.

Where is he?

Pause.

I think it's my birthday soon.

Pause.

No, no. No, no. I sleep like other people. No more no less. Why should I? If I sleep late my mother wakes me up. There are things to do.

Pause.

If I have been asleep, why hasn't Mummy woken me up?

HORNBY I have woken you up.

DEBORAH But I don't know you.

Pause.

Where is everyone? Where is my dog? Where are my sisters? Last night Estelle was wearing my dress. But I said she could.

Pause.

I am cold.

HORNBY How old are you?

DEBORAH I am twelve. No. I am sixteen. I am seven.

Pause.

I don't know. Yes. I know. I am fourteen. I am fifteen. I'm lovely fifteen.

Pause.

You shouldn't have brought me here. My mother will ask me where I've been.

Pause.

You shouldn't have touched me like that. I shan't tell my mother. I shouldn't have touched you like that.

Pause.

Oh Jack.

Pause.

It's time I was up and about. All those dogs are making such a racket. I suppose Daddy's feeding them. Is Estelle going to marry that boy from Townley Street? The ginger boy? Pauline says he's got nothing between his ears. Thick as two planks. I've given it a good deal of rather more mature thought and I've decided she should not marry him. Tell her not to marry him. She'll listen to you.

Pause.

Daddy?

HORNBY She didn't marry him.

DEBORAH Didn't?

Pause.

It would be a great mistake. It would ruin her life.

HORNBY She didn't marry him.

Silence.

DEBORAH I've seen this room before. What room is this? It's not my bedroom. My bedroom has blue lilac on the walls. The sheets are soft, pretty. Mummy kisses me.

Pause.

This is not my bedroom.

HORNBY You have been in this room for a long time. You have been asleep. You have now woken up.

DEBORAH You shouldn't have brought me here. What are you saying? Did I ask you to bring me here? Did I make eyes at you? Did I show desire for you? Did I let you peep up my skirt? Did I flash my teeth? Was I as bold as brass? Perhaps I've forgotten.

HORNBY I didn't bring you here. Your mother and father brought you here.

DEBORAH My father? My mother?

Pause.

Did they bring me to you as a sacrifice? Did they sacrifice me to you?

Pause.

No, no. You stole me…in the night.

Pause.

Have you had your way with me?

HORNBY I am here to take care of you.

DEBORAH They all say that.

Pause.

You've had your way with me. You made me touch you. You stripped me. I cried…but…but it was my lust made me cry. You are a devil. My lust was my own. I kept it by me. You took it from me. Once open never closed. Never closed again. Never closed always open. For eternity. Terrible. You have ruined me.

Pause.

I sound childish. Out of...tune.

Pause.

How old am I?

Pause.

Eighteen?

HORNBY No.

DEBORAH Well then, I've no idea how old I am. Do you know?

HORNBY Not exactly.

DEBORAH Why not?

Pause.

My sisters would know. We're very close. We love each other. We're known as the three bluebells.

Pause.

Why is everything so quiet? So still? I'm in a sandbag. The sea. Is that what I hear? A long way away. Gulls. Haven't heard a gull for ages. God what a racket. Where's Pauline? She's such a mischief. I have to keep telling her not to be so witty. That's what I say. You're too witty for your own good. You're so sharp you'll cut yourself. You're too witty for your own tongue. You'll bite your own tongue off one of these days and I'll keep your tongue in a closed jar and you'll never ever ever ever be witty again.

Pause.

She's all right, really. She just talks too much. Whereas Estelle is as deep as a pond. She's marvellous at crossing her legs. Sen-su-al.

Pause.

This is a hotel. A hotel near the sea. Hastings? Torquay? There's more to this than meets the eye. I'm coming to that conclusion. There's something very shady about you. Pauline always says I'll end up as part of the White Slave Traffic.

Pause.

Yes. This is a white tent. When I open the flap I'll step out into the Sahara Desert.

HORNBY You've been asleep.

DEBORAH Oh, you keep saying that! What's wrong with that? Why shouldn't I have a long sleep for a change? I need it. My body demands it. It's quite natural. I may have overslept but I didn't do it deliberately. If I had any choice in the matter I'd much prefer to be up and about. I love the morning. Why do you blame me? I was simply obeying the law of the body.

HORNBY I know that. I'm not blaming you.

DEBORAH Well, how long have I been asleep?

Pause.

HORNBY You have been asleep for twenty-nine years.

Silence.

DEBORAH You mean I'm dead?

HORNBY No.

DEBORAH I don't feel dead.

HORNBY You're not.

DEBORAH But you mean I've been dead?

HORNBY If you had been dead you wouldn't be alive now.

DEBORAH Are you sure?

HORNBY No one wakes from the dead.

DEBORAH No, I shouldn't think so.

Pause.

Well, what was I doing if I wasn't dead?

HORNBY We don't know...what you were doing.

DEBORAH We?

Pause.

Where's my mother? My father? Estelle? Pauline?

HORNBY Pauline is here. She's waiting to see you.

DEBORAH She shouldn't be out at this time of night. I'm always telling her. She needs her beauty sleep. Like I do, by the way. But of course I'm her elder sister so she doesn't listen to me. And Estelle doesn't listen to me because she's my elder sister. That's family life. And Jack? Where's Jack? Where's my boyfriend? He's my boyfriend. He loves me. He loves me. I once saw him cry. For love. Don't make him cry again. What have you done to him? What have you done with him? What? What? What?

HORNBY Be calm. Don't agitate yourself.

DEBORAH Agitate myself?

HORNBY There's no hurry about any of this.

DEBORAH Any of what?

HORNBY Be calm.

DEBORAH I am calm.

Pause.

I've obviously committed a criminal offence and am now in prison. I'm quite prepared to face up to the facts. But what offence? I can't imagine what offence it could be. I mean one that would bring...such a terrible sentence.

HORNBY This is not a prison. You have committed no offence.

DEBORAH But what have I done? What have I been doing? Where have I been?

HORNBY Do you remember nothing of where you've been? Do you remember nothing...of all that has happened to you?

DEBORAH Nothing has happened to me. I've been nowhere.

Silence.

HORNBY I think we should—

DEBORAH I certainly don't want to see Pauline. People don't want to see their sisters. They're only sisters. They're so witty. All I hear is chump chump. The side teeth. Eating everything in sight. Gold chocolate. So greedy eat it with the paper on. Munch all the ratshit on the sideboard. Someone has to polish it off. Been there for years. Statues of excrement. Wrapped in gold. I've never got used to it. Sisters are diabolical. Brothers are worse. One day I prayed I would see no one ever again, none of them ever again. All that eating, all that wit.

Pause.

HORNBY I didn't know you had any brothers.

DEBORAH What?

Pause.

HORNBY Come. Rest. Tomorrow...is another day.

DEBORAH No it isn't. No it isn't. It is not! *(She smiles)* Yes, of course it is. Of course it is. Tomorrow is another day. I'd love to ask you a question.

HORNBY Are you not tired?

DEBORAH Tired? Not at all. I'm wide awake. Don't you think so?

HORNBY What is the question?

DEBORAH How did you wake me up?

Pause.

Or did you not wake me up? Did I just wake up myself? All by myself? Or did you wake me with a magic wand?

HORNBY I woke you with an injection.

DEBORAH Lovely injection. Oh how I love it. And am I beautiful?

HORNBY Certainly.

DEBORAH And you are my Prince Charming. Aren't you?

Pause.

Oh speak up.

Pause.

Silly shit. All men are alike.

Pause.

I think I love you.

HORNBY No, you don't.

DEBORAH Well, I'm not spoilt for choice here, am I? There's not another man in sight. What have you done with all the others? There's a boy called Peter. We play with his trains, we play... Cowboys and Indians... I'm a tomboy. I knock him about. But that was...

Pause.

But now I've got all the world before me. All life before me. All my life before me.

Pause.

I've had enough of this. Find Jack. I'll say yes. We'll have kids. I'll bake apples. I'm ready for it. No point in hanging about. Best foot forward. Mummy's motto. Bit of a cheek, I think, Mummy not coming in to say hello, to say goodnight, to tuck me up, to sing me a song, to warn me about going too far with boys. Daddy I love but he is a bit absent-minded. Thinking of other things. That's what Pauline says. She says he has a mistress in Fulham. The bitch. I mean Pauline. And she's only…thirteen. I keep telling her I'm not prepared to tolerate her risible, her tendentious, her eclectic, her ornate, her rococo insinuations and garbled inventions. I tell her that every day of the week.

Pause.

Daddy is kind and so is Mummy. We all have breakfast together every morning in the kitchen. What's happening?

Pause.

HORNBY One day suddenly you stopped.

DEBORAH Stopped?

HORNBY Yes.

Pause.

You fell asleep and no one could wake you. But although I use the word sleep, it was not strictly sleep.

DEBORAH Oh, make up your mind!

Pause.

You mean you thought I was asleep but I was actually awake?

HORNBY Neither asleep nor awake.

DEBORAH Was I dreaming?

HORNBY Were you?

DEBORAH Well was I? I don't know.

Pause.

I'm not terribly pleased about all this. I'm going to ask a few questions in a few minutes. One of them might be: What did I look like while I was asleep, or while I was awake, or whatever it was I was? Bet you can't tell me.

HORNBY You were quite still. Fixed. Most of the time.

DEBORAH Show me.

Pause.

Show me what I looked like.

He demonstrates a still, fixed position. She studies him. She laughs, stops abruptly.

Most of the time? What about the rest of the time?

HORNBY You were taken for walks twice a week. We encouraged your legs to move.

Pause.

At other times you would suddenly move of your own volition very quickly, very quickly indeed, spasmodically, for short periods, and as suddenly as you began you would stop.

Pause.

DEBORAH Did you ever see...tears...well in my eyes?

HORNBY No.

DEBORAH And when I laughed...did you laugh with me?

HORNBY You never laughed.

DEBORAH Of course I laughed. I have a laughing nature.

Pause.

Right. I'll get up now.

He moves to her.

No! Don't! Don't be ridiculous.

She eases herself out of the bed, stands, falls. He moves to her.

No! Don't! Don't! Don't! Don't touch me.

She stands, very slowly. He retreats, watching. She stands still, begins to walk, in slow motion, towards him.

Let us dance.

She dances, by herself, in slow motion.

I dance.

She dances.

I've kept in practice, you know. I've been dancing in very narrow spaces. Kept stubbing my toes and bumping my head. Like Alice. Shall I sit here? I shall sit here.

She sits at the table. He joins her. She touches the arms of her chair, touches the table, examines the table.

I like tables, don't you? This is a rather beautiful table. Any chance of a dry sherry?

HORNBY Not yet. Soon we'll have a party for you.

DEBORAH A party? For me? How nice. Lots of cakes and lots of booze?

HORNBY That's right.

DEBORAH How nice.

Pause.

Well, it's nice at this table. What's the news? I suppose the war's still over?

HORNBY It's over, yes.

DEBORAH Oh good. They haven't started another one?

HORNBY No.

DEBORAH Oh good.

Pause.

HORNBY You danced in narrow spaces?

During the following, **PAULINE** *enters.*

DEBORAH Oh yes. The most crushing spaces. The most punishing spaces. That was tough going. Very difficult. Like dancing with someone dancing on your foot all the time, I mean *all* the time, on the same spot, just slam, slam, a big boot on your foot, not the most ideal kind of dancing, not by a long chalk. But sometimes the space opened and became light, sometimes it opened and I was so light, and when you feel so light you can dance till dawn and I danced till dawn night after night, night after night…for a time… I think…until…

She has become aware of the figure of **PAULINE**, *standing in the room. She stares at her.* **PAULINE** *is a woman in her early forties.*

PAULINE Deborah.

DEBORAH *stares at her.*

Deborah. It's Pauline. *(She turns to* **HORNBY***)* She's looking at me. *(She turns back to* **DEBORAH***)* You're looking at me. Oh Deborah…you haven't looked at me…for such a long time.

Pause.

I'm your sister. Do you know me?

DEBORAH *laughs shortly and turns away.* **HORNBY** *stands and goes to* **PAULINE**.

HORNBY I didn't call you.

PAULINE *regards him.*

Well, all right. Speak to her.

PAULINE What shall I say?

HORNBY Just talk to her.

PAULINE Doesn't it matter what I say?

HORNBY No.

PAULINE I can't do her harm?

HORNBY No.

PAULINE Shall I tell her lies or the truth?

HORNBY Both.

Pause.

PAULINE You're trembling.

HORNBY Am I?

PAULINE Your hand.

HORNBY Is it? *(He looks at his hand)* Trembling? Is it? Yes.

PAULINE *goes to* **DEBORAH**, *sits with her at the table.*

PAULINE Debby. I've spoken to the family. Everyone was so happy. I spoke to them all, in turn. They're away, you see. They're on a world cruise. They deserve it. It's been so hard for them. And Daddy's not too well, although in many respects he's as fit as a fiddle, and Mummy... It's a wonderful trip. They passed through the Indian Ocean. And the Bay of Bosphorus. Can you imagine? Estelle also...needed a total break. It's a wonderful trip. Quite honestly, it's the trip of a lifetime. They've stopped off in Bangkok. That's where I found them. I spoke to them all, in turn. And they all send so much love to you. Especially Mummy.

Pause.

I spoke by radio telephone. Shore to ship. The captain's cabin. Such excitement.

Pause.

Tell me. Do you...remember me?

DEBORAH *stands and walks to her bed, in slow motion. Very slowly she gets into the bed. She lies against the pillows, closes her eyes. She opens her eyes, looks at* **PAULINE**, *beckons to her.* **PAULINE** *goes to the bed.*

DEBORAH Let me look into your eyes. *(She looks deeply into* **PAULINE**'s *eyes)* So you say you're my sister?

PAULINE I am.

DEBORAH Well, you've changed. A great deal. You've aged... substantially. What happened to you? *(She turns to* **HORNBY***)* What happened to her? Was it a sudden shock? I know shocks can age people overnight. Someone told me. *(She turns to* **PAULINE***)* Is that what happened to you? Did a sudden shock age you overnight?

PAULINE No it was you—

PAULINE *looks at* **HORNBY**. *He looks back at her, impassive.* **PAULINE** *turns back to* **DEBORAH**.

It was you. You were standing with a vase of flowers in your hands. You were about to put it down on the table. But you didn't put it down. You stood still, with the vase in your hands, as if you were...fixed. I was with you, in the room. I looked into your eyes.

Pause.

I said: "Debby?"

Pause.

But you remained...quite...still. I touched you. I said: "Debby?" Your eyes were open. You were looking nowhere. Then you suddenly looked at me and saw me and smiled at me and put the vase down on the table.

Pause.

But at the end of dinner, we were all laughing and talking, and Daddy was making jokes and making us laugh, and you said you couldn't see him properly because of the flowers in the middle of the table, where you had put them, and you stood and picked up the vase and you took it towards that little sidetable by the window, walnut, and Mummy was laughing and even Estelle was laughing and then we suddenly looked at you and you had stopped. You were standing with the vase by the sidetable, you were about to put it down, your arm was stretched towards it but you had stopped.

Pause.

We went to you. We spoke to you. Mummy touched you. She spoke to you.

Pause.

Then Daddy tried to take the vase from you. He could not... wrench it from your hands. He could not...move you from the spot. Like...marble.

Pause.

You were sixteen.

DEBORAH *turns to* **HORNBY**.

DEBORAH She must be an aunt I never met. One of those distant cousins. *(To* **PAULINE***)* Have you left me money in your Will? Well, I could do with it.

PAULINE I'm Pauline.

DEBORAH Well, if you're Pauline you've put on a remarkable amount of weight in a very short space of time. I can see you're not keeping up with your ballet classes. My God! You've grown breasts! *(She stares at* **PAULINE***'s breasts and suddenly looks down at herself)*

PAULINE We're women.

DEBORAH Women?

HORNBY You're a grown woman, Deborah.

DEBORAH *(to* **PAULINE***)* Is Estelle going to marry that ginger boy from Townley Street?

HORNBY Deborah. Listen. You're not listening.

DEBORAH To what?

HORNBY To what your sister has been saying.

DEBORAH *(to* **PAULINE***)* Are you my sister?

PAULINE Yes. Yes.

DEBORAH But where did you get those breasts?

PAULINE They came about.

> **DEBORAH** *looks down at herself.*

DEBORAH I'm slimmer. Aren't I?

PAULINE Yes.

DEBORAH Yes. I'm slimmer.

> *Pause.*

I'm going to run into the sea and fall into the waves. I'm going to rummage about in all the water.

Pause.

Are we going out to dinner tonight?

Pause.

Where's Jack? Tongue-tied as usual. He's too shy for his own good. And Pauline's so sharp she'll cut herself. And Estelle's such a flibbertigibbet. I think she should marry that ginger boy from Townley Street and settle down before it's too late.

Pause.

PAULINE I am a widow.

DEBORAH This woman is mad.

HORNBY No. She's not.

Pause.

She has been coming to see you regularly...for a long time. She has suffered for you. She has never forsaken you. Nor have I.

Pause.

I have been your doctor for many years. This is your sister. Your father is blind. Estelle looks after him. She never married. Your mother is dead.

Pause.

It was I who took the vase from your hands. I lifted you on to this bed, like a corpse. Some wanted to bury you. I forbade it. I have nourished you, watched over you, for all this time.

Pause.

I injected you and woke you up. You will ask why I did not inject you twenty-nine years ago. I'll tell you. I did not possess the appropriate fluid.

Pause.

You see, you have been nowhere, absent, indifferent. It is we who have suffered.

Pause.

You do see that, I'm sure. You were an extremely intelligent young girl. All opinions confirm this. Your mind has not been damaged. It was merely suspended, it took up a temporary habitation...in a kind of Alaska. But it was not entirely static, was it? You ventured into quite remote...utterly foreign... territories. You kept on the move. And I charted your itinerary. Or did my best to do so. I have never let you go.

Silence.

I have never let you go.

Silence.

I have lived with you.

Pause.

Your sister Pauline was twelve when you were left for dead. When she was twenty I married her. She is a widow. I have lived with you.

Silence.

DEBORAH I want to go home.

Pause.

I'm cold. *(She takes* **PAULINE***'s hand)* Is it my birthday soon? Will I have a birthday party? Will everyone be there? Will they all come? All our friends? How old will I be?

PAULINE You will. You will have a birthday party. And everyone will be there. All your family will be there. All your old friends. And we'll have presents for you. All wrapped up... wrapped up in such beautiful paper.

DEBORAH What presents?

PAULINE Ah, we're not going to tell you. We're not going to tell you that. Because they're a secret.

Pause.

Think of it. Think of the thrill...of opening them, of unwrapping them, of taking out your presents and looking at them.

DEBORAH Can I keep them?

PAULINE Of course you can keep them. They're your presents. They're for you...only.

DEBORAH I might lose them.

PAULINE No, no. We'll put them all around you in your bedroom. We'll see that nobody else touches them. Nobody will touch them. And we'll kiss you goodnight. And when you wake up in the morning your presents...

Pause.

DEBORAH I don't want to lose them.

PAULINE They'll never be lost. Ever.

Pause.

And we'll sing to you. What will we sing?

DEBORAH What?

PAULINE We'll sing "Happy Birthday" to you.

Pause.

DEBORAH Now what was I going to say? *(She begins to flick her cheek, as if brushing something from it)* Now what —? Oh dear, oh no. Oh dear.

Pause.

Oh dear. *(The flicking of her cheek grows faster)* Yes, I think they're closing in. They're closing in. They're closing the walls in. Yes. *(She bows her head, flicking faster, her fingers now moving about over her face)* Oh...well...oooohhhhh... oh no...oh no... *(During the course of this speech her body becomes hunch-backed)* Let me out. Stop it. Let me out. Stop it. Stop it. Stop it. Shutting the walls on me. Shutting them down on me. So tight, so tight. Something panting, something panting. Can't see. Oh, the light is going. The light is going. They're shutting up shop. They're closing my face. Chains and padlocks. Bolting me up. Stinking. The smell. Oh my goodness, oh dear, oh my goodness, oh dear, I'm so young. It's a vice. I'm in a vice. It's at the back of my neck. Ah. Eyes stuck. Only see the shadow of the tip of my nose. Shadow of the tip of my nose. Eyes stuck. *(She *stops flicking abruptly, sits still. Her body straightens. She looks up. She looks at her fingers, examines them)* Nothing.

Silence. She speaks calmly, is quite still.

Do you hear a drip?

Pause.

I hear a drip. Someone's left the tap on.

Pause.

I'll tell you what it is. It's a vast series of halls. With enormous interior windows masquerading as walls. The windows are mirrors, you see. And so glass reflects glass. For ever and ever.

Pause.

You can't imagine how still it is. So silent I hear my eyes move.

Silence.

I'm lying in bed. People bend over me, speak to me. I want to say hello, to have a chat, to make some inquiries. But you can't do that if you're in a vast hall of glass with a tap dripping.

Silence. She looks at **PAULINE**.

I must be quite old. I wonder what I look like. But it's of no consequence. I certainly have no intention of looking into a mirror.

Pause.

No.

She looks at **HORNBY**.

You say I have been asleep. You say I am now awake. You say I have not awoken from the dead. You say I was not dreaming then and am not dreaming now. You say I have always been alive and am alive now. You say I am a woman.

She looks at **PAULINE**, *then back to* **HORNBY**.

She is a widow. She doesn't go to her ballet classes any more. Mummy and Daddy and Estelle are on a world cruise. They've stopped off in Bangkok. It'll be my birthday soon. I think I have the matter in proportion.

Pause.

Thank you.

Curtain.

FURNITURE AND PROPERTY LIST

Onstage: Bed. *On it:* white bedclothes, pillows
Table
2 chairs
Window

Offstage: Nil

LIGHTING PLOT

Property fittings required: nil

To open: general interior lighting

Cue 1   **Deborah:** "Thank you."   (Page 23)
       Blackout

EFFECTS PLOT

No cues

VISIT THE SAMUEL FRENCH BOOKSHOP AT THE ROYAL COURT THEATRE

Browse plays and theatre books, get expert advice and enjoy a coffee

Samuel French Bookshop
Royal Court Theatre
Sloane Square
London
SW1W 8AS
020 7565 5024

Shop from thousands of titles on our website

 samuelfrench.co.uk

 samuelfrenchltd

 samuel french uk

www.ingramcontent.com/pod-product-compliance
Lightning Source LLC
Chambersburg PA
CBHW070454050426
42450CB00012B/3266